CALM YOUR
CHAOS

TRANSFORMING OVERTHINKING INTO YOUR SUPERPOWER

By D.R. Riley

Copyright © 2024 by Torment Publishing. All rights reserved.

All rights reserved. This book or any portion thereof
may not be reproduced or used in any manner whatsoever
without the express written permission of the publisher
except for the use of brief quotations in a book review.

Printed in the United States of America

Riley, D.R.
Calm Your Chaos: Transforming Overthinking into Your
Superpower

For more information on reproducing sections of this book or sales
of this book, go to www.tormentpublishing.com

Contents:

Chapter 1: The Overthinking Epidemic

Hey there, fellow overthinker! If you're reading this, chances are your brain is spinning faster than a hamster on an energy drink-fueled wheel. Don't worry, you're not alone in this mental marathon. Welcome to the Overthinking Club—where we turn molehills into mountains and spend more time in hypothetical scenarios than in reality!

But here's the kicker: overthinking is like trying to solve a Rubik's cube in the dark. You keep twisting and turning, but you're not getting anywhere. Sound familiar? Of course it does! That's why you picked up this book, right?

Now, let's get real for a second. Overthinking isn't just some quirky personality trait. It's a full-blown epidemic, and it's spreading faster than cat videos on the internet. It's the invisible enemy that's keeping you up at night, making you second-guess every decision, and turning your mind into a 24/7 worry factory.

But hey, don't panic! (I know, I know, easier said than done for us overthinkers.) The fact that you're reading this means you're already taking the first step towards mental freedom. Go ahead, give yourself a high-five! You deserve it.

Let me share a little story with you. When I was in my twenties, I was the poster child for overthinking. My friends had planned a casual dinner, and I wasn't involved in choosing the restaurant. Cue the mental gymnastics! I spent hours spiraling, convinced they'd left me out of the decision-making on purpose. "Do they even want me there?" "Am I not important enough to ask?" "What if they're all closer to each other than they are to me?"

By the time I arrived at the restaurant, I was a bundle of nerves. I second-guessed every interaction, overanalyzed every laugh, and felt like an outsider in my own friend group. My anxiety was so obvious that my friends started treating me differently—they walked on eggshells, unsure of what to say. The very thing I feared—being left out—was becoming a reality, all because of my overthinking.

The kicker? I later found out they'd chosen the restaurant spontaneously, with no big discussion. All that worry for nothing! But the damage was done. My overthinking had created an awkward vibe that lasted for weeks. Talk about a self-fulfilling prophecy, right?

This scenario illustrates how overthinking can affect our social relationships, potentially turning unfounded fears into real issues. It also shows how our internal thoughts can manifest in our behavior, influencing how others perceive and interact with us.

But here's the thing: overthinking isn't just about wasted time. It's a sneaky thief that robs you of joy, peace, and sometimes even relationships. It's like having a backseat driver in your head, constantly yelling conflicting directions. No wonder we're all feeling a bit lost!

So, what's the game plan? Well, buckle up, buttercup, because we're about to embark on a mind-bending journey. We're going to dive deep into the overthinking ocean, swim with the anxiety sharks, and come out the other side with a treasure chest of strategies to calm that chaotic cranium of yours.

In this book, we'll explore:

1. The nitty-gritty of overthinking (spoiler alert: your brain isn't broken, it's just a bit overenthusiastic)

2. The sneaky ways overthinking sabotages your life (it's not just about being indecisive, trust me)

3. Practical strategies to tame your wild thoughts (no, we're not going to suggest you live in a cave)

4. How to transform your overthinking into a superpower (yes, you read that right!)

But before we dive in, I want you to do something for me. Take a deep breath. No, deeper than that. I want you to breathe so deeply that your belly button says hello to your spine. Feel better? Good. Remember this feeling, because we'll be coming back to it a lot.

Now, here's your first mission, should you choose to accept it (and let's face it, you've probably already overthought whether you should or not): For the next 24 hours, I want you to become an Overthinking Detective. Notice when your thoughts start spiraling.

Don't judge them, just observe. It's like birdwatching, but for anxious thoughts.

Write down what triggers your overthinking. Is it work? Relationships? That weird noise your car is making? Keep a tally. You might be surprised at what you discover.

Remember, awareness is the first step to change. You can't fix a problem if you don't know it exists. And trust me, by the end of this book, you'll not only be aware of your overthinking, you'll be the CEO of your own thoughts.

So, are you ready to turn your mind from a chaotic mess into a well-oiled thinking machine? Are you prepared to trade in your "what ifs" for "why nots"? Then let's do this! It's time to go from overthinker to over-achiever.

Stay tuned, because in the next chapter, we're going to put your brain under the microscope and figure out why it's running like it's training for a mental marathon. Spoiler alert: it's not because you watched too much TV as a kid (though your mom might disagree).

Remember, you've got this. And even if you don't think you've got this, well, that's just your overthinking talking. We'll show it who's boss soon enough!

Chapter 2: Understanding Your Mind - The Overthinking Factory

Welcome back, fellow thought-jugglers! In the last chapter, we identified the overthinking epidemic and I gave you your first mission: to become an Overthinking Detective. As you embark on that 24-hour journey of noticing your thought patterns, let's dive deeper into understanding why our minds work the way they do. This knowledge will enhance your detective work and give you a framework for interpreting what you observe.

Now, let's explore that beautiful, complicated, sometimes frustrating organ between your ears. It's time to understand why your brain loves to play on repeat more than your favorite playlist.

First things first: your brain isn't broken. It's just... enthusiastic. Like that friend who always brings way too much food to a party. It's trying to help, really!

Let me take you back to my late 20s. Picture this: a slightly younger me, sitting in my first grown-up apartment, staring at my phone. My best friend hadn't texted back in three hours. Cue the overthinking tornado!

"Did I say something wrong?"

"Is she mad at me?"

"Maybe she's hanging out with other friends and doesn't want me to know."

"What if she's decided she doesn't want to be friends anymore?"

By the time my friend finally texted back (she'd been in a movie, phone off), I'd mentally ended our friendship, moved to a new city, and changed my name. Okay, maybe not that last part, but you get the idea.

This scenario probably feels familiar to many of you. Maybe your Overthinking Detective exercise will reveal similar patterns. Perhaps you noticed that social situations, work pressures, or personal insecurities were your primary triggers. Whatever you discovered, pat yourself on the back. Awareness is the first step towards change.

So, why does our brain do this? Well, buckle up, because we're about to get a little sciency (don't worry, I promise to keep it more 'Bill Nye' than 'Nobel Prize').

Your brain, in all its infinite wisdom, evolved to keep you safe. Back in the caveman days, overthinking might've kept you from becoming a saber-toothed tiger's lunch. "Hmm, is that rustle in the bushes the wind, or am I about to be an appetizer?" The cautious overthinkers survived to pass on their genes. Congratulations, you're the product of successful worriers!

But here's the thing: while our environment has changed drastically, our brains are still running the old software. They're trying to protect us from tigers in a world where the biggest threats are usually deadlines, social media likes, and whether or not we remembered to put deodorant on this morning.

Your brain is like an overprotective parent, always imagining the worst-case scenario. It's that voice saying, "Don't forget your jacket, what if it rains? And snows? And then there's a freak heatwave followed by a locust plague?" It means well, but sometimes it needs to chill.

Now, let's talk about cognitive biases. These are like the brain's shortcuts, and boy, do they love to feed overthinking. Here are a few of my personal favorites:

Catastrophizing: Always jumping to the worst possible conclusion. Like that time in my early 30s when my boss said "We need to talk," and I convinced myself I was getting fired, blacklisted, and possibly deported (I'm a citizen, by the way).

Mind Reading: Assuming you know what others are thinking. Spoiler alert: unless you're Professor X, you don't.

Emotional Reasoning: Believing that if you feel something, it must be true. "I feel like a failure, therefore I am a failure." Newsflash: feelings aren't facts!

Overgeneralization: Taking one negative experience and applying it to all future scenarios. "I bombed one presentation, so I'm terrible at public speaking and should never do it again."

Black and White Thinking: Seeing things in extremes with no middle ground. "If I'm not perfect, I'm a complete failure."

Understanding these biases is like getting the cheat codes to your brain. Once you recognize them, you can start to challenge them.

Let's dig deeper into how these biases might show up in your Overthinking Detective exercise. As you observe your thoughts, keep an eye out for these common patterns. You might catch yourself catastrophizing about a small mistake at work, turning a minor error into a career-ending disaster in your mind. Or perhaps you'll notice yourself mind-reading, assuming a friend is upset with you because their text seemed short.

These patterns are incredibly common, and recognizing them is a huge step. It's like finally seeing the Matrix—suddenly, you're aware of the underlying code that's been influencing your thoughts all along.

But awareness alone isn't enough. We need to actively work on challenging these thought patterns. That's where our next mission comes in.

Here's your assignment for this chapter: Bias Bingo! As you continue your Overthinking Detective work, let's add another layer. For the next week, try to catch yourself falling into these thinking traps. When you notice one, call it out (maybe not out loud in public, unless you enjoy confused stares). The more aware you become of these patterns, the more power you have to change them.

Create a little chart or use your phone's notes app. Each time you catch a bias, mark it down. At the end of the week, see which ones show up most often. This isn't about judging yourself—it's about gathering intel. You're a scientist studying the fascinating specimen that is your own mind!

Remember, your brain isn't the enemy. It's more like a well-meaning but slightly neurotic friend. Our goal isn't to silence it, but to turn down its volume from "heavy metal concert" to "background coffee shop chatter."

As you go through this week, be kind to yourself. Recognizing these patterns can be uncomfortable at first. You might feel discouraged when you realize how often these biases pop up. But remember—this discomfort is a sign of growth. You're developing a new awareness, and that's huge!

In my early 30s, when I first started recognizing my own thought patterns, it felt overwhelming. I remember thinking, "Wow, my brain really likes to assume the worst, doesn't it?" But as I kept at it, something magical happened. The very act of noticing these patterns started to change them. It was like shining a light on the monsters under the bed—once I could see them clearly, they weren't quite so scary anymore.

Alright, my fellow thought-wranglers, it's time for some tough love. Put this book down. Yes, you heard me right. Close it, set it aside, and go live your life for a day or two. Why? Because reading without doing is like watching workout videos while eating ice cream—entertaining, but not exactly transformative.

Look, I get it. It's tempting to keep reading, to devour all this juicy info in one sitting. But trust me, rushing through without doing the exercises is like trying to learn swimming by reading about it. You might know the theory, but you'll still sink when you hit the water.

So here's what I want you to do: Take your time. Do the Overthinking Detective exercise. Play some Bias Bingo. Really dive into these experiences. Yes, just reading this book will help change your mindset, but the exercises? They're where the magic happens. They're what will transform you from an overthinking hot mess to a cool, calm, collected thought master.

When you come back to this book (and I know you will, you awesome overachiever), we'll start exploring practical strategies to tame that overactive mind of yours. We'll take the awareness you're building now and turn it into action.

Remember, be kind to that beautiful, complex brain of yours. It's doing its best, even if its best sometimes feels like running a marathon in your mind. Now go out there and do your homework. I'll be here waiting, ready to guide you on the next leg of your journey from overthinker to over-achiever. You've got this!

Chapter 3: Staying Out of the Black Hole

Welcome back, brave thought explorers! I hope you've had a chance to put on your detective hat and do some serious thought-watching. If you're anything like I was when I first started this journey, you might be feeling a mix of enlightenment and overwhelm right now. That's perfectly normal. In fact, it's a great sign that you're making progress!

Let's start by unpacking what you might have discovered during your Overthinking Detective work and Bias Bingo game. Did you notice how often your thoughts spiraled into worst-case scenarios? Or how frequently you assumed you knew what others were thinking? Don't worry if you found yourself doing this a lot—we all do. The important thing is that you're now aware of it.

When I was in my late 20s, I remember doing a similar exercise and being shocked at how often I catastrophized. I'd see my boss frowning and immediately jump to "I'm getting fired." A friend wouldn't text back for a few hours, and I'd conclude our friendship was over. It was like my brain was constantly preparing for doomsday!

But here's the thing: awareness is the first step to change. Now that you can see these patterns, you have the power to interrupt them. It's like catching a snowball at the top of a hill before it turns into an avalanche.

So, how do we stop that snowball? How do we stay out of the overthinking black hole that threatens to suck us in? Let's dive into some strategies.

1. The Pause Button Technique

Imagine your brain has a pause button. Whenever you catch yourself spiraling into overthinking, hit that button. Take a deep breath. In that pause, ask yourself:

- Is this thought helpful?
- Is it based on facts or assumptions?
- What would I tell a friend who had this thought?

This simple act of pausing can be incredibly powerful. It creates a space between stimulus and response, giving you the chance to choose your reaction rather than being swept away by it.

For example, let's say you're waiting for an important email. An hour passes, then two, then three. Your mind starts racing:

"They hate my proposal."
"I'm going to lose this opportunity."
"I'll never succeed in this field."

Pause. Breathe. Now, let's apply our questions:

- Is this thought helpful? (Not really, it's just making me anxious.)
- Is it based on facts or assumptions? (Assumptions. I don't actually know why they haven't responded yet.)
- What would I tell a friend? (Probably that there could be many reasons for the delay, and to be patient.)

See how that changes things? Suddenly, the black hole doesn't seem so threatening.

2. The Reality Check

Our brains are excellent at imagining the worst, but they're not always great at assessing probability. That's where the reality check comes in.

When you catch yourself catastrophizing, ask:

- What's the worst that could happen?
- What's the best that could happen?
- What's most likely to happen?

Let's apply this to a real-life scenario. In my early 30s, I was preparing for a big presentation at work. The night before, my brain went into overdrive:

Worst case: I'd stumble over my words, forget everything, get fired, become homeless, and end up living in a cardboard box.

Best case: I'd give the presentation of the century, get an immediate promotion, and be headhunted by a Fortune 500 company on the spot.

Most likely: I'd do okay. There might be a few stumbles, but overall, it would be fine.

Guess what? The most likely scenario was pretty much exactly what happened. By acknowledging this, I was able to calm my nerves and sleep that night.

3. The Thought Ladder

Sometimes, our thoughts get stuck at the bottom of a very negative ladder. The thought ladder technique helps us climb up to more balanced, realistic thoughts.

Start by writing down your most negative thought. Then, try to come up with slightly less negative thoughts, working your way up to neutral and then positive thoughts.

For example:

Bottom rung: "I'm a complete failure at relationships."

Next rung: "I've had some challenges in relationships."

Middle rung: "Relationships are difficult for many people."

Higher rung: "I've learned from my past relationships."

Top rung: "I have the potential to build a healthy relationship."

This technique helps you see that there's a spectrum of thoughts, not just extremes.

4. The 'So What?' Strategy

This is a personal favorite of mine. When you find yourself overthinking, ask yourself "So what?" and keep asking until you get to the root fear.

For instance:

"I made a mistake at work."
So what?
"My boss might be mad at me."
So what?
"I might get a bad performance review."
So what?
"I might not get a raise."
So what?
"I'm afraid of financial insecurity."

Ah, there it is. Now we know what's really bothering you, and you can address that core fear directly.

5. The Future Self Perspective

When you're caught in an overthinking spiral, it can feel like your current situation is eternal. That's where the future self perspective comes in handy.

Ask yourself: "Will this matter in a day? A week? A month? A year?"

Often, you'll find that the thing you're obsessing over won't even be a blip on your radar in the not-so-distant future.

I remember agonizing over a typo in an important email I sent in my late 20s. I was convinced it would ruin my professional reputation forever. Now, I can't even remember what the typo was or who the email was to. Perspective is everything.

Implementing These Strategies

Now, I know what you're thinking. "These strategies sound great, but how do I remember to use them when I'm in the throes of overthinking?"

Great question! Here are a few tips:

1. Set reminders: Use your phone to set random reminders throughout the day to check in with your thoughts.
2. Use visual cues: Put sticky notes with key phrases like "Pause," "Reality Check," or "So What?" in places you'll see often.
3. Practice, practice, practice: The more you use these techniques, the more automatic they'll become.
4. Be patient with yourself: You're learning a new skill. It takes time.
5. Celebrate small wins: Every time you catch yourself overthinking and apply one of these strategies, give yourself a mental high-five.

Remember, the goal isn't to never overthink again. That's about as realistic as never having a bad hair day. The goal is to catch yourself sooner, pull yourself out faster, and reduce the frequency and intensity of overthinking episodes.

Your Homework

Yes, there's more homework! Don't groan—this is the good kind of homework. For the next week, I want you to choose one of these strategies and really focus on implementing it. Keep a journal of when you use it, what triggered your overthinking, and how the strategy helped.

At the end of the week, reflect on your experiences. What worked well? What was challenging? How do you feel compared to before you started this exercise?

Remember, change doesn't happen overnight. It's a process, and you're already making great strides by being aware and taking action.

In our next chapter, we'll explore how to harness the power of your overthinking and turn it into a superpower. Yes, you read that right—we're going to take this "flaw" and make it work for you!

Until then, keep practicing, stay curious about your thought patterns, and most importantly, be kind to yourself. You're doing great work, and I'm proud of you for taking these steps to improve your mental well-being.

Now, go forth and conquer those thoughts! You've got this, and I'll be here cheering you on every step of the way.

Chapter 4: Crushing It – Turning Overthinking into Your Superpower

If you've made it this far, give yourself a pat on the back. You're not just reading—you're doing the work, and that's what separates the overthinkers from the over-achievers.

Now, I know what you might be thinking: "Wait a minute, I thought we were trying to stop overthinking. Now you're telling me it's a superpower?" Alright, let's fasten our mental seatbelts, because we're about to flip the script on everything you thought you knew about your overactive mind.

Remember back in Chapter 2 when we talked about how our caveman ancestors' overthinking kept them from becoming saber-toothed tiger snacks? Well, that same mental machinery that's been driving you nuts can actually be your secret weapon—if you know how to use it.

Time to put your thinking cap on turbo mode! Let me take you back to my early 30s when I was planning a surprise birthday party for my mom's 60th. Naturally, my brain went into overdrive. I was imagining every possible thing that could go wrong, every potential pitfall, every worst-case scenario. Sound familiar?

But here's where things get interesting. Instead of trying to shut down those thoughts, I decided to channel them. I grabbed a notebook and started writing down every concern my overactive mind could conjure up. And you know what? By the time I was done, I had inadvertently created the most comprehensive party plan my family had ever seen.

I'd thought of everything: backup venues in case of bad weather, alternative meal options for guests with newly discovered allergies, entertainment for the kids so the adults could relax, and even a contingency plan for if Mom found out about the surprise. I'd even prepared a speech with multiple versions to suit different emotional reactions she might have.

When the big day came, everything went off without a hitch. One of my brothers was amazed. "How did you think of all these details?" he asked. I just smiled and said, "It's a gift."

And that, my friends, is when I realized: overthinking, when harnessed properly, is indeed a superpower.

So, how do we transform our overthinking from a burden into a blessing? Let's dive in.

Reframe Your Overthinking

The first step is to change how you view your overthinking. Instead of seeing it as a problem to be solved, try viewing it as a tool to be utilized. Your overactive mind isn't a glitch—it's a feature!

Exercise: The next time you catch yourself overthinking, instead of trying to stop it, say to yourself, "Okay, brain, what valuable insights are you trying to give me?" Then, write down whatever comes to mind. You might be surprised at the creative solutions or important considerations you uncover.

Channel Your Overthinking into Preparation

Overthinkers are often exceptionally well-prepared. Why? Because they've already thought through every possible scenario!

For example, when I was planning our 10th wedding anniversary celebration in my mid-30s, my overthinking went into overdrive. "What if the romantic beach picnic gets rained out? What if the surprise serenade I arranged cancels last minute? What if my wife suddenly develops an allergy to the flowers I've ordered?" (Okay, I didn't actually think of that last one, but you get the idea.)

Instead of letting these thoughts stress me out, I used them to create the most detailed anniversary plan my wife had ever seen (not that she saw it beforehand, of course). I had backup plans for our backup plans. There was an indoor location secured in case of rain, a playlist ready if the serenade fell through, and even a selection of non-floral gifts just in case. And guess what? When a few things did go wrong on the big day - the beach was unexpectedly closed for maintenance and our favorite restaurant lost our reservation - we were more than ready to handle them. We ended up having a cozy indoor picnic followed by stargazing from our backyard, and my wife said it was the most thoughtful anniversary yet. Overthinking for the win!

Exercise: Think of an upcoming event or project you're worried about. Set a timer for 15 minutes and write down every possible thing that could go wrong. Then, spend another 15 minutes brainstorming solutions for each potential problem. Congratulations! You've just turned your overthinking into excellent preparation.

Use Overthinking for Creative Problem-Solving

Overthinkers often excel at seeing connections and possibilities that others miss. This can be an incredible asset in creative fields or when tackling complex problems.

In my late 30s, I was stuck on a difficult writing project. My overthinking mind kept spinning out different scenarios and plot twists. Instead of getting frustrated, I started jotting down these ideas. Many were outlandish, but hidden among them were some genuinely innovative concepts that ended up transforming my story.

Exercise: Next time you're faced with a problem, embrace your overthinking. Let your mind run wild with possible solutions, no matter how far-fetched. Write them all down. Then, review your list. You might find that combining elements from different ideas leads to a brilliant solution you wouldn't have considered otherwise.

Empathy and Emotional Intelligence

Overthinkers often have a knack for understanding others' perspectives and anticipating their needs. This can translate into high emotional intelligence and strong interpersonal skills.

I once had a coworker who always seemed to know exactly what to say in difficult situations. When I asked her secret, she laughed and said, "Oh, I just spend way too much time imagining every possible way a conversation could go." Sound familiar?

Exercise: In your next interaction, consciously use your overthinking to consider the other person's perspective. What might they be thinking or feeling? How could your words or actions impact them? Use these insights to communicate more effectively and empathetically.

Attention to Detail

Overthinkers often notice details that others miss. This can be invaluable in many professions, from editing to quality control to detective work.

In my first job out of college, I was often teased for being too meticulous. But when my attention to detail caught a major error that saved the company thousands of dollars, suddenly my "overthinking" was seen in a new light.

Exercise: Pick an everyday object and spend five minutes examining it in detail. What do you notice that you've never seen before? Practice applying this level of attention to your work or hobbies.

Turning Anxiety into Excitement

Here's a mind-blowing fact: physiologically, anxiety and excitement are almost identical. The only real difference is how we label the feeling.

So, the next time you feel that familiar overthinking anxiety creeping in, try this: Instead of telling yourself to calm down, tell yourself you're excited. "I'm excited to tackle this challenge." "I'm excited to see how this turns out."

It might feel weird at first, but research shows this simple reframing can significantly improve performance and well-being.

Exercise: For the next week, whenever you notice yourself feeling anxious about something, consciously relabel it as excitement. Keep a journal of how this impacts your thoughts and performance.

The Power of "Yet"

Overthinkers often get caught up in what they perceive as their limitations. "I'm not good at public speaking." "I can't handle confrontation." Here's where the power of "yet" comes in.

Add "yet" to the end of these statements. "I'm not good at public speaking... yet." "I can't handle confrontation... yet." This simple addition transforms a fixed mindset into a growth mindset, opening up possibilities for improvement.

Exercise: Write down three things you believe you can't do. Now, add "yet" to each statement. Spend some time reflecting on how this changes your perception of these challenges.

Remember, the goal isn't to eradicate your overthinking—it's to harness it. Like any superpower, it takes practice to control. There will still be times when your thoughts spiral, and that's okay. Use the techniques we've learned in previous chapters to bring yourself back, then see if you can channel that mental energy into something productive.

Your Homework

This week, I want you to actively look for opportunities to use your overthinking as a superpower. Keep a "Superpower Journal" where you record instances where your overthinking led to a positive outcome. Maybe it helped you prepare thoroughly for a meeting, or gave you insight into a friend's behavior, or helped you catch a mistake before it became a problem.

At the end of the week, review your journal. I bet you'll be surprised at how often your overthinking actually worked in your favor.

When you are ready to move on, in our next chapter, we'll explore how to maintain your progress and prevent relapse into uncontrolled overthinking. But for now, go forth and embrace your superpower! Remember, with great overthinking comes great responsibility (and potentially great achievements).

Until next time, keep those thoughts flowing, but now with purpose and direction. You're not just an overthinker anymore—you're a super-thinker in training!

Chapter 5: Knock It Off! Avoiding the Debuffs

Welcome back, super-thinkers in training! By now, you've learned to recognize your overthinking patterns, developed strategies to stay out of the mental black hole, and even started to harness your overthinking as a superpower. But let's face it—old habits die hard. It's time to talk about how to maintain your progress and avoid slipping back into the overthinking abyss.

Think of your newfound overthinking management skills like a video game character's power-ups. You've leveled up, gained new abilities, and are ready to take on the boss levels of life. But just like in games, there are always debuffs lurking around the corner, waiting to sap your strength and send you back to square one.

Let's identify these debuffs and learn how to dodge them like a pro!

Debuff #1: The Comfort Zone Trap

Remember how cozy it felt to wallow in your overthinking? There's a strange comfort in familiar anxiety, isn't there? It's like that ratty old sweater you know you should throw out but keep wearing anyway.

I'll let you in on a secret: In my early 30s, I caught myself deliberately overthinking just because it felt familiar. I'd finally gotten a handle on my anxiety, and suddenly, I felt... lost. Who was I without my constant worry?

Don't fall for this trap! Recognize that discomfort is a sign of growth. Embrace it. Your new, calmer self isn't a stranger—it's the real you, finally breaking free.

Exercise: Write a letter to your overthinking self. Thank it for trying to protect you all these years, but explain that you've got new tools now. Keep this letter handy for moments when you feel the urge to slip back into old patterns.

Debuff #2: The All-or-Nothing Fallacy

You've been doing great, using your new strategies, feeling more in control. Then bam! You have one bad day of spiraling thoughts, and suddenly you think, "I've failed. I'll never get better at this."

Whoa there, partner! Progress isn't linear. You wouldn't expect to bench press 300 pounds after a week at the gym, would you? Managing your thoughts is a skill, and like any skill, it takes consistent practice.

I remember the first time I slipped after weeks of progress. I catastrophized about catastrophizing! Meta-overthinking, if you will. But then I reminded myself: setbacks are part of the journey, not the end of it.

Exercise: Create a "Progress Journal." Each day, write down one small win in managing your thoughts. On tough days, flip through this journal to remind yourself how far you've come.

Debuff #3: The Comparison Trap

In this age of carefully curated social media lives, it's easy to fall into the comparison trap. "Look at how zen and together everyone else is! Why am I still struggling?"

Let me let you in on a little secret: everyone is struggling with something. Those perfectly posed Instagram yogis? I bet they overthink their hashtags.

Remember, you're seeing everyone else's highlight reel while living your own behind-the-scenes. It's not a fair comparison.

Exercise: Next time you find yourself playing the comparison game, try this: List three things you've overcome or improved in your thought patterns. Focus on competing with yourself, not others.

Debuff #4: The Perfectionism Paralysis

Ah, perfectionism—the overthinking overachiever's favorite frenemy. You might think, "If I can't do this perfectly, why bother at all?"

I'll tell you why: because done is better than perfect.

In my late 30s, I almost didn't start my own business because I was waiting for the "perfect" time, with the "perfect" plan. Spoiler alert: there's no such thing. I finally had to embrace the mantra "Progress over perfection" to take the leap.

Exercise: Set a timer for 10 minutes and work on a task you've been putting off because you couldn't do it "perfectly." When the timer goes off, stop. Congratulate yourself on the progress, no matter how small.

Debuff #5: The "I Don't Have Time" Illusion

"I'm too busy to meditate/journal/practice these techniques." Sound familiar? Here's the truth: you don't find time, you make time.

Your mental health is just as important as that urgent work project or social obligation. In fact, managing your overthinking will likely make you more efficient in all areas of life.

I used to think I was too busy to take breaks. Then I realized that my "busy-ness" was often just spinning my mental wheels. Taking time to reset actually made me more productive.

Exercise: Identify one "time-waster" in your day (mindless social media scrolling, perhaps?). Replace it with a 5-minute overthinking management exercise. Do this every day for a week and see how it impacts your overall mindset.

Maintaining Your Progress

Now that we've identified the debuffs, let's talk about how to keep your overthinking management skills sharp:

1. Daily Check-ins: Take a few minutes each day to assess your thought patterns. Are you slipping into old habits? Catch them early!

2. Celebrate Small Wins: Did you catch yourself catastrophizing and turn it around? That's a win! Acknowledge and celebrate these moments.

3. Practice Self-Compassion: Be kind to yourself on the tough days. Remember, you're rewiring years of thought patterns. It takes time.

4. Stay Connected: Share your journey with a trusted friend or join a support group. Sometimes, just knowing you're not alone can be incredibly powerful.

5. Keep Learning: Your brain loves novelty. Continue to seek out new strategies and information about managing overthinking. (But don't let this turn into a new form of overthinking—balance is key!)

Your Homework

This week, I want you to create a "Maintenance Plan" for your overthinking management. Include:

- Daily practices (like meditation or journaling)
- Weekly check-ins
- Strategies for handling setbacks
- A list of go-to techniques for when you feel overwhelmed
- Rewards for hitting milestones in your progress

Remember, this journey isn't about reaching a destination where you never overthink again. It's about building a toolkit that allows you to navigate life's challenges with greater ease and confidence.

You've come so far already, and I'm incredibly proud of you. Keep flexing those mental muscles, dodge those debuffs, and remember—you've got this!

In our next chapter, we'll explore how to apply all these skills in real-life, high-stress situations. Get ready to put your newfound superpowers to the test!

Until then, keep thinking, but now with purpose and direction. You're not just managing your overthinking anymore—you're mastering it!

Chapter 6: Real Life, Real Examples

Alright, thought tamers, it's showtime! You've been training in the mental gym, flexing those cognitive muscles, and now it's time to step out onto the main stage of life. You've got a toolkit full of shiny new strategies, and your overthinking is transforming from a pesky gremlin into a powerful ally. But how does all this mental magic translate to the real world? Grab your popcorn (or perhaps a stress ball), because we're about to watch your new superpowers in action on the big screen of everyday life.

In this chapter, we're going to take a break from exercises and homework. Instead, let's explore some real-life scenarios where these skills come into play. Think of this as your chance to sit back, relax, and see your new superpowers in action.

Scenario 1: The Job Interview

Picture this: You've landed an interview for your dream job. Exciting, right? But as the day approaches, your mind goes into overdrive:

"What if I forget everything I know?"
"What if I spill coffee on my shirt?"
"What if they hate me?"

Sound familiar? Let's see how our newfound skills can help:

First, employ the Pause Button Technique. Take a deep breath. Now, let's do a Reality Check:

Worst case: You don't get this particular job.

Best case: You nail the interview and get the job of your dreams.

Most likely: You do okay. There might be a few stumbles, but overall, it goes fine.

Remember, this is just one opportunity. Your worth isn't determined by a single interview.

Next, use your overthinking as a superpower. Channel that energy into thorough preparation. Research the company, prepare answers to common questions, and come up with thoughtful questions of your own.

By the time you walk into that interview, you're not just prepared—you're over-prepared, in the best way possible. And guess what? The interviewer is impressed by your thoughtful questions and in-depth knowledge of the company.

Scenario 2: The First Date

Ah, the classic overthinking minefield. You've agreed to a first date, and suddenly your brain is working overtime:

"What if we run out of things to talk about?"
"What if I laugh at the wrong moment?"
"What if they don't like me?"

Time to put those skills to work:

Start with the 'So What?' Strategy. Keep asking "So what?" until you get to the root fear. Often, it's something like "I'm afraid of rejection" or "I'm worried about being alone."

Now that you've identified the core fear, you can address it directly. Remind yourself that your worth isn't determined by one person's opinion of you.

Use the Future Self Perspective. Will this one date matter in a year? Five years? Probably not.

Channel your overthinking into empathy. Use your ability to consider multiple perspectives to be a great listener and conversationalist.

The result? You go into the date more relaxed, genuinely curious about the other person, and ready to enjoy the experience for what it is—a chance to connect with another human being.

Scenario 3: The Big Project

You've been assigned a major project at work. It's a great opportunity, but also a bit overwhelming. Your mind starts racing:

"What if I'm not up to the task?"
"What if I miss a crucial detail?"

"What if I let everyone down?"

Let's tackle this:

First, reframe your overthinking. Instead of seeing it as anxiety, view it as excitement. You're not nervous about the project; you're excited about the challenge!

Use your overthinking for creative problem-solving. Let your mind explore all the possible approaches to the project. Write them down, no matter how outlandish they seem at first.

Apply your attention to detail to break the project down into manageable tasks. Your thoroughness ensures that no aspect of the project is overlooked.

The outcome? You deliver a comprehensive, innovative project that exceeds expectations. Your boss is impressed not just with the result, but with your foresight in anticipating and addressing potential issues before they arose.

Scenario 4: The Family Gathering

Family gatherings can be a hotbed for overthinking. As the annual reunion approaches, your thoughts start spiraling:

"What if Uncle Bob brings up politics again?"

"What if Aunt Susan comments on my weight?"

"What if I say the wrong thing and upset everyone?"

Time to put your skills to work:

Use the Thought Ladder technique. Start with your most negative thought and work your way up to more balanced, realistic thoughts.

Prepare, but don't over-prepare. Have a few neutral topics in mind for conversation, but don't script out every interaction.

Remember your empathy superpower. Everyone at the gathering might be dealing with their own anxieties and overthinking. Approach interactions with compassion.

The result? You navigate the family gathering with grace, deflecting potentially contentious topics and fostering positive interactions. You might even enjoy yourself!

In all these scenarios, the key is to recognize when you're overthinking, pause, apply your strategies, and then channel that mental energy productively. You're not trying to eliminate thoughts—you're learning to direct them.

Remember, progress isn't about perfection. There will still be times when overthinking gets the better of you, and that's okay. The goal is progress, not perfection.

You've got a powerful set of tools at your disposal now. With practice, applying these techniques will become second nature. You're not just managing your overthinking anymore—you're mastering it and using it to your advantage.

In our next chapter, we'll look at how to maintain these skills over the long term and how to handle setbacks when they occur. But for now, take a moment to appreciate how far you've come. You're not just surviving your thoughts anymore—you're thriving because of them.

Until next time, keep those thoughts flowing, but now with purpose and direction. You've got this!

54

Chapter 7: Five Awesome Weapons For Success

Congratulations, mental ninjas! You've made it to the advanced class. By now, you're not just surviving the overthinking obstacle course—you're doing backflips through it. But even the most skilled thought-wranglers need to keep their tools sharp. Think of this chapter as your high-tech arsenal against overthinking, complete with shiny gadgets that would make James Bond jealous.

1: The Mindfulness Magnet

Imagine a magnet that pulls your mind back to the present moment whenever it starts time-traveling to the land of "what ifs." That's mindfulness in a nutshell. It's like a GPS for your brain, constantly recalibrating to "You Are Here."

I remember when I first tried mindfulness. I sat down, closed my eyes, and promptly started planning my grocery list. But with practice, I learned to notice my thoughts without getting caught up in them. It was like watching clouds pass by instead of getting swept up in the storm.

Try this: Next time you're brushing your teeth, focus entirely on the sensation. Feel the bristles, taste the toothpaste, hear the sound. When your mind wanders (and it will), gently bring it back. Congratulations! You've just had a mindfulness moment.

2: The Gratitude Cannon

This weapon blasts away negative thoughts with a powerful beam of appreciation. It's hard to spiral into worry when you're focused on what's going right.

In my early 30s, I started ending each day by noting three things I was grateful for. At first, it felt cheesy. But soon, I found myself looking for good things throughout the day, just so I'd have something to write down. My overthinking brain, once a worry factory, became a gratitude-seeking missile.

3: The Perspective Periscope

This tool lets you pop your head above the murky waters of overthinking and see the bigger picture. It's like zooming out on Google Earth— suddenly, that hill you've been struggling to climb looks like a tiny bump on a vast landscape.

I use this when I'm catastrophizing about a small mistake. I ask myself, "Will this matter in a year? In five years?" Usually, the answer is no. Suddenly, that typo in an email doesn't seem so life-ending.

4: The Action Activator

This gadget transforms overthinking energy into productive action. It's like a mental alchemist, turning lead thoughts into golden deeds.

When I find myself overthinking a problem, I ask, "What's one small step I can take right now?" Maybe it's sending that email I've been procrastinating on, or making that doctor's appointment I've been putting off. Taking action, no matter how small, breaks the overthinking cycle.

5: The Self-Compassion Shield

This is your force field against self-criticism. It deflects those harsh, judgmental thoughts and replaces them with understanding and kindness.

I used to berate myself for overthinking. "Why can't you just relax?" I'd think, adding another layer of stress. Learning self-compassion was like giving myself permission to be human. Now, when I catch myself overthinking, I think, "It's okay, this is just your mind trying to protect you. Let's find a better way to do that."

These five weapons aren't just theoretical—they're practical tools you can use every day. The more you practice, the more natural they'll feel. Soon, you'll be wielding them like a thought-taming superhero.

Remember, the goal isn't to eliminate overthinking completely. It's to have a well-stocked arsenal so you can choose the right tool for each situation. Some days you'll be a master strategist, other days you might fumble a bit. That's okay—you're human, not a robot.

As we wrap up this chapter, I want you to take a deep breath and relax those brain muscles. You might be thinking, "Wow, that's a lot of new techniques to remember!" But here's the beautiful thing—you don't have to memorize it all right now.

Think of this book as your personal mental mindset manual. It's not a one-time read, but a trusty reference guide you can return to whenever you need a refresher. Like a Swiss Army knife for your mind, you've got all these tools at your fingertips. You don't need to use every tool every day, but they're here when you need them.

Maybe today you'll flex your Gratitude Cannon, and tomorrow you'll polish your Perspective Periscope. The point is, you're building a toolkit, not cramming for a test. There's no pressure to be perfect—just progress.

So, keep this book handy. Flip through it when you're feeling stuck, or when you need a pep talk from your future self. Let it be your go-to guide for navigating the twists and turns of your thought patterns.

Remember, you're not just managing your thoughts—you're evolving your mindset. And like any good evolution, it happens gradually, one small change at a time.

In our next chapter, we'll dive into how overthinking affects our relationships and social situations. We'll explore strategies to navigate these complex interpersonal waters with more confidence and less mental turmoil. But for now, give yourself a pat on the back. You're not just reading—you're equipping yourself with a versatile toolkit for clearer, calmer thinking in all areas of your life.

Keep growing, keep learning, and remember: your overthinker's mind isn't a problem to be solved—it's a power to be harnessed!

Chapter 8: Overthinking in Relationships and Social Situations

Ah, relationships—the fertile soil where overthinking grows like weeds after a spring rain. If you've ever spent hours analyzing a text message or replayed a conversation in your head until it's more worn out than your favorite sweater, congratulations! You're a card-carrying member of the Overthinking in Relationships Club.

But fear not, fellow overthinkers! We're about to shine a spotlight on these relationship mind-traps and equip you with the tools to navigate them like a pro.

The Romantic Rollercoaster

Let's start with romantic relationships—the ultimate playground for our overactive minds. Remember my first date story from earlier chapters? Well, buckle up, because we're diving deeper.

In my late 20s, I met someone who seemed perfect. We had a great first date, and then... radio silence for three days. Cue the overthinking tornado:

"Did I say something wrong?"
"Maybe they're just not that into me."
"What if they met someone else?"
"I knew I shouldn't have ordered the garlic bread!"

Sound familiar? Here's the thing: while we're spinning out these scenarios, our partner is probably just living their life, blissfully unaware of the mental gymnastics we're performing.

Strategy: The Reality Check

When you find yourself on this romantic rollercoaster, it's time for a reality check. List out your assumptions, then challenge them with facts. For example:

Assumption: "They haven't texted because they don't like me."
Fact: They said they had a busy week at work.
Fact: They seemed to enjoy our date and suggested meeting again.
Fact: Not everyone texts every day, especially early in dating.

By grounding yourself in facts, you can slow down that runaway thought train.

The Friendship Frenzy

Friendships aren't immune to overthinking either. Have you ever sent a message to a group chat, saw that everyone read it, but no one responded? Cue the internal panic:

"Did I say something offensive?"
"Maybe they're talking about me in another chat."
"I knew I should have used a different emoji!"

Strategy: The Perspective Flip

Try this: imagine your friend was the one who sent the message, and you got busy and forgot to respond. Would you want them spiraling into self-doubt? Probably not. Extend the same grace to yourself that you'd give to a friend.

The Family Feud

Family relationships can be an overthinking minefield. Whether it's preparing for a holiday gathering or navigating complex family dynamics, our minds can go into overdrive.

I once spent weeks stressing about telling my parents I was changing careers. I imagined every possible negative reaction, rehearsed my explanations countless times, and nearly talked myself out of it entirely.

Strategy: The "So What?" Technique

When you find yourself catastrophizing about family situations, employ the "So What?" technique we learned earlier. Keep asking "So what?" until you get to the root of your fear. Often, you'll find it's not as scary as your mind made it out to be.

The Social Media Spiral

Ah, social media—the modern-day fuel for overthinking. You post a photo, and it doesn't get as many likes as you expected. Or worse, you see your friends having fun without you. The overthinking begins:

"Why didn't they invite me?"
"Do people not like my posts anymore?"
"Am I just not interesting enough?"

Strategy: The Digital Detox

Sometimes, the best strategy is to step away. Try a mini digital detox. Set specific times to check social media, and stick to them. Use the extra time to connect with people in real life or pursue a hobby. You might be surprised at how much clearer your thoughts become when they're not clouded by the digital noise.

Universal Strategies for Relationship Overthinking

1. Communication is Key: Often, the antidote to overthinking in relationships is honest communication. If something's bothering you, speak up (calmly and kindly).

2. Practice Self-Compassion: Remember, everyone has moments of insecurity and doubt. Be as kind to yourself as you would be to a friend.

3. Focus on What You Can Control: You can't control others' thoughts or actions, but you can control your own. Focus your energy there.

4. Mindfulness in Interactions: Practice being fully present in your interactions. You'll be amazed at how much overthinking diminishes when you're truly engaged in the moment.

5. Celebrate the Good: Make a conscious effort to acknowledge and appreciate the positive aspects of your relationships. Gratitude is a powerful antidote to negative overthinking.

Remember, perfect relationships don't exist—not even in those carefully curated Instagram posts. What does exist are real, messy, beautiful connections between imperfect humans. Your overthinking mind is just trying to protect you, but with these strategies, you can teach it to relax a little.

In our next chapter, we'll tackle overthinking in the workplace and academic settings. But for now, take a deep breath and give yourself a pat on the back. You're not just surviving the relationship overthinking jungle—you're learning to thrive in it.

Keep those thoughts flowing, but now with more understanding and less judgment. You've got this!

Chapter 9: Conquering Overthinking at Work and in Academia

Welcome to the professional overthinking arena, where deadlines loom, expectations soar, and your mind runs laps around the office (or classroom) faster than the office gossip spreads. Whether you're climbing the corporate ladder or hitting the books, overthinking can turn your career or academic journey into a mental obstacle course. But fear not! We're about to turn your overthinking tendencies into your secret weapon for success.

The Imposter Syndrome Tango

Let's kick things off with everyone's favorite workplace dance: the Imposter Syndrome Tango. You know the steps - you've achieved success, but you're convinced it's all a fluke and any minute now, someone's going to discover you're a fraud.

I remember my first big presentation as a department lead. Despite weeks of preparation, I was certain I'd be exposed as a complete novice. My inner dialogue went something like this:

"They're going to realize I have no idea what I'm talking about."
"What if I freeze up and forget everything?"
"They probably regret hiring me already."

Sound familiar? Here's how to break this toxic tango:

Strategy: The Evidence Collection

Become a detective of your own success. Collect tangible evidence of your achievements and competencies. Keep a "wins" folder in your email or a journal where you record positive feedback and accomplishments. When imposter syndrome strikes, review your evidence. It's hard to argue with facts!

The Decision Paralysis Polka

In the workplace and academia, decisions are as common as coffee runs. But for overthinkers, each choice can feel like defusing a bomb. Should you take on that new project? Which research topic should you choose for your thesis? Cue the mental merry-go-round:

"What if I make the wrong choice?"
"What if I'm not capable of handling this?"
"What if this decision ruins my entire career/academic future?"

Strategy: The Worst-Case Scenario Reframe

Instead of avoiding the worst-case scenario, lean into it. Ask yourself:
1. What's the absolute worst that could happen?
2. How likely is that to actually occur?
3. If it did happen, how would I handle it?

Often, you'll find that even the worst-case scenario is manageable, and the chances of it happening are slim. This can help you move from paralysis to action.

The Perfectionism Paradox

Ah, perfectionism - the favorite flavor of overthinking for many high achievers. Whether it's obsessing over every word in an email or rewriting your thesis introduction for the 47th time, perfectionism can be a productivity killer.

Strategy: The Good Enough Goal

Set a "good enough" goal for each task. Decide what level of quality is necessary and sufficient, then stop when you reach it. Remember, done is often better than perfect, especially in fast-paced work and academic environments.

The Feedback Freak-Out

Receiving feedback, whether it's a performance review or graded assignment, can send an overthinker into a tailspin. Every comment becomes a judgment on your worth as a human being.

Strategy: The Feedback Reframe

Try this: view feedback as a gift. It's information that can help you improve, not a verdict on your value. When you receive feedback, ask yourself:
1. What can I learn from this?
2. How can I use this to grow?
3. What specific actions can I take based on this feedback?

The Test Anxiety Tango

For students (and professionals taking certifications), test anxiety can be overwhelming. Your mind races through every possible scenario except the one where you actually remember what you studied.

Strategy: The Mental Rehearsal

Use your vivid imagination to your advantage. Spend time visualizing yourself taking the test calmly and confidently. Imagine yourself recalling information easily, managing your time well, and feeling relaxed. This mental rehearsal can help reduce anxiety and improve performance.

Universal Strategies for Work and Academic Overthinking:

1. The Pomodoro Technique: Break your work into 25-minute focused sessions, followed by 5-minute breaks. This can prevent the overthinking spiral and boost productivity.

2. The Worry Schedule: Allocate a specific time each day for worrying about work or school. When worries pop up outside this time, note them down for later.

3. The Mentorship Method: Find a mentor or study buddy. Sometimes, an outside perspective can cut through the overthinking fog.

4. The Celebration Checklist: At the end of each day, write down three things you accomplished, no matter how small. This shifts your focus from what you're worrying about to what you're achieving.

5. The Growth Mindset Mantra: Adopt a phrase like "I'm learning and improving every day" to counter perfectionist tendencies.

Remember, your overthinking mind in professional and academic settings is often just trying to help you succeed. It's like an overeager intern - full of energy but needing some guidance. With these strategies, you can channel that mental energy into real productivity and growth.

In our next chapter, we'll explore how mindfulness and present-moment living can further calm your overthinking tendencies. But for now, take a moment to appreciate how far you've come. You're not just surviving in your professional or academic world - you're learning to thrive, one thought at a time.

Keep those synapses firing, but now with more focus and less fretting. Life is good... and so are you!

Chapter 10: Mindfulness and Present-Moment Living

Alright, mental time travelers, it's time to make a pit stop in the present moment. If you're an overthinker, your mind probably spends more time wandering through the halls of "what if" than hanging out in the "what is." But fear not! We're about to turn your mind from a time machine into a comfy hammock in the here and now.

The Present Moment: It's a Gift, That's Why It's Called the Present

(I know, I know, but I couldn't resist the dad joke.)

Mindfulness isn't just a buzzword thrown around by yoga instructors and meditation apps. It's a powerful tool for overthinkers like us. At its core, mindfulness is about paying attention to the present moment without judgment. Sounds simple, right? Well, for us overthinkers, it can feel about as easy as herding cats.

The Overthinking Time Warp

Let's paint a picture. You're sitting down to enjoy a meal, but instead of tasting your food, your mind is replaying this morning's awkward elevator conversation and planning tomorrow's presentation. By the time you tune back in, your plate is empty and you can't remember a single bite.

Or maybe you're out for a walk, but instead of noticing the trees or the breeze, you're mentally drafting emails and worrying about your to-do list. Sound familiar?

This is the overthinking time warp, where we're physically in one place but mentally everywhere else. It's exhausting, and it robs us of the joy and peace available in the present moment.

The Mindfulness Rescue Mission

So how do we beam ourselves back to the present? Here are some strategies to get you started:

1. The Five Senses Check-In

This is my go-to technique for quick mindfulness. Wherever you are, whatever you're doing, take a moment to notice:
- 5 things you can see
- 4 things you can touch
- 3 things you can hear
- 2 things you can smell
- 1 thing you can taste

This simple exercise anchors you in the present moment and can interrupt the overthinking spiral.

2. The Breath Anchor

Your breath is always with you (hopefully), making it a perfect mindfulness tool. Try this:
- Take a deep breath in for a count of 4
- Hold for a count of 4
- Exhale for a count of 4
- Hold for a count of 4
- Repeat

Focus on the sensation of your breath. When your mind wanders (and it will), gently bring it back to your breath.

3. The Body Scan

Start at your toes and work your way up to the top of your head, noticing any sensations in each part of your body. This practice not only brings you into the present but can also help you identify where you're holding tension.

4. The Mindful Mundane

Choose a routine activity—brushing your teeth, washing dishes, or even eating—and do it mindfully. Notice every sensation, every movement. This turns everyday tasks into mindfulness practices.

5. The Nature Nurture

Spend time in nature, really noticing your surroundings. The sounds of birds, the feel of the wind, the patterns in tree bark. Nature has a way of pulling us into the present moment.

The "But My Mind Won't Shut Up" Conundrum

Now, I know what you're thinking (because I'm an overthinker too, remember?). "But what if I can't stop my thoughts? What if I'm bad at mindfulness?"

Here's the secret: The goal of mindfulness isn't to stop thinking. It's to notice your thoughts without getting caught up in them. Think of your thoughts as clouds passing through the sky of your mind. You're not trying to stop the clouds; you're learning to watch them float by without hopping on for a ride.

The Present Moment Payoff

Practicing mindfulness and present-moment living doesn't just feel good—it has real benefits for overthinkers:

1. Reduced Anxiety: When we're focused on the present, we're not worrying about the future or ruminating on the past.
2. Improved Focus: Regular mindfulness practice can enhance our ability to concentrate and avoid distractions.
3. Better Emotional Regulation: By observing our thoughts and feelings without judgment, we can respond to situations more calmly.
4. Enhanced Creativity: Being present can help us tap into our creative flow more easily.
5. Improved Relationships: When we're truly present with others, our connections deepen.

My Mindfulness Journey

When I first tried mindfulness, I thought I was doing it wrong. My mind was like a hyperactive puppy, constantly darting from one thought to another. But with practice (and patience), I started to have moments of real presence.

I remember the first time I truly tasted a meal mindfully. It was like I'd been eating in black and white all my life, and suddenly everything was in vibrant color. The textures, the flavors, the aromas—it was a whole new experience.

Your Mindfulness Mission

Your mission, should you choose to accept it (and I really hope you do), is to practice one mindfulness technique each day for the next week. It doesn't have to be long—even 5 minutes a day can make a difference.

Remember, mindfulness is a practice. Some days will feel easier than others, and that's okay. The goal isn't perfection; it's progress.

As we wrap up this chapter, take a moment right now to check in with yourself. Notice your breath, the sensation of your body in your chair, the sounds around you. Congratulations! You've just taken a step towards a more mindful, present-focused life.

In our next chapter, we'll explore how cultivating self-compassion can further soothe your overthinking mind. But for now, enjoy this moment. After all, it's the only one we ever truly have.

Keep breathing, keep noticing, and remember: the present moment is where life happens. Your overthinking mind will thank you for the mini-vacation!

Chapter 11: Cultivating Self-Compassion and Healthy Habits

It's time to turn that razor-sharp mind of yours away from self-criticism and toward self-compassion. If your inner voice is usually more drill sergeant than cheerleader, you're not alone. But what if I told you that being kinder to yourself could actually be the key to taming your overthinking beast?

The Self-Criticism Trap

Let's start with a little self-reflection. How do you talk to yourself when you make a mistake? If your inner dialogue sounds something like this:

"You idiot, how could you mess that up?"
"Everyone else has it together. What's wrong with you?"
"You'll never get it right. Why even try?"

Then congratulations (or should I say, my condolences?), you've fallen into the self-criticism trap. It's like being stuck in a mental escape room where all the clues are insults.

The Problem with Being Your Own Worst Critic

Here's the kicker: all that self-criticism? It's actually fuel for your overthinking fire. When we're harsh with ourselves, we trigger our brain's threat response. And what does an overthinking brain do when it feels threatened? It goes into overdrive, trying to problem-solve its way out of the perceived danger.

Enter: Self-Compassion

Self-compassion isn't about letting yourself off the hook or lowering your standards. It's about treating yourself with the same kindness you'd offer a good friend. It's recognizing that being human means being imperfect, and that's okay.

Dr. Kristin Neff, a pioneer in self-compassion research, breaks it down into three components:

1. Self-kindness vs. Self-judgment
2. Common humanity vs. Isolation
3. Mindfulness vs. Over-identification

Let's break these down and see how they can help us overthinkers:

1. Self-kindness vs. Self-judgment

Instead of berating yourself for overthinking, try comforting yourself. "It's okay that I'm overthinking right now. This is hard, but I'm doing my best."

2. Common humanity vs. Isolation

Remember, you're not alone in your overthinking. Millions of people struggle with this. It's part of the human experience, not a personal failing.

3. Mindfulness vs. Over-identification

This is where our mindfulness practice comes in handy. Notice your thoughts without getting caught up in them. "I'm having the thought that I'm a failure" is very different from "I am a failure."

The Self-Compassion Break

Here's a quick exercise you can use anytime you catch yourself in a self-critical spiral:

1. Acknowledge the difficulty: "This is a moment of suffering."

2. Recognize the common humanity: "Suffering is a part of life. I'm not alone in this."

3. Offer yourself kindness: Place your hand on your heart and say, "May I be kind to myself in this moment."

Healthy Habits: The Foundation of a Calmer Mind

Now that we've addressed the inner world, let's talk about the outer world. Your physical habits have a huge impact on your mental state. Here are some key areas to focus on:

1. Sleep: The Overthinker's Kryptonite

If you're not getting enough quality sleep, your overthinking tendencies will be in overdrive. Some tips for better sleep:

- Stick to a consistent sleep schedule
- Create a relaxing bedtime routine
- Limit screen time before bed
- Keep your bedroom cool and dark

2. Nutrition: Fuel for Your Brain

What you eat affects how you think. Some brain-friendly foods include:

- Fatty fish (rich in omega-3s)
- Berries (high in antioxidants)
- Nuts and seeds (good source of vitamin E)
- Dark chocolate (in moderation, for the flavonoids)

3. Exercise: The Natural Thought-Tamer

Regular physical activity can be a powerful antidote to overthinking. It doesn't have to be intense—even a daily walk can make a big difference.

4. Hydration: Keep Your Brain Juicy

Dehydration can affect your mood and cognitive function. Keep a water bottle handy and sip throughout the day.

5. Digital Detox: Give Your Brain a Break

Constant connectivity can fuel overthinking. Try setting aside some screen-free time each day to let your mind rest.

The Habit-Forming Hack

Forming new habits can be tough, especially for us overthinkers who might obsess over doing it "perfectly." Here's a simple hack: the "Two-Minute Rule."

If a habit takes less than two minutes to do, do it without hesitation. Floss one tooth. Meditate for two minutes. Write one sentence in your journal. Starting small builds momentum and bypasses the overthinking that often prevents us from starting at all.

My Self-Compassion Journey

I used to think self-compassion was self-indulgent. But when I started practicing it, I noticed something surprising: the kinder I was to myself, the less I overthought. It was like my brain finally felt safe enough to relax.

I remember the first time I consciously practiced self-compassion after a big mistake at work. Instead of spiraling into self-criticism and anxiety, I took a deep breath and told myself, "This is hard, but you're doing your best. Everyone makes mistakes sometimes." The relief was immediate and profound.

Your Self-Compassion and Healthy Habits Mission

This week, I challenge you to:

1. Practice the self-compassion break at least once a day.

2. Choose one healthy habit to focus on. Remember, start small!

3. Notice how these practices affect your overthinking tendencies.

Remember, cultivating self-compassion and healthy habits is a journey, not a destination. There will be ups and downs, and that's okay. The goal is progress, not perfection.

As we wrap up this chapter, take a moment to appreciate yourself for doing this work. You're not just reading—you're actively working to improve your mental well-being. That's pretty amazing, don't you think?

Now, here's a radical idea: put this book down for a few days. Yes, you heard me right! Take some time to digest what you've learned so far. Practice the techniques we've discussed. Live with them. See how they fit into your daily life.

Rome wasn't built in a day, and neither is a calmer mind. Give yourself the gift of time to implement these strategies without the pressure of moving on to the next chapter right away. Remember, this isn't a race. It's about real, lasting change.

When you feel ready—and only then—come back for our next chapter, where we'll explore strategies for navigating major life decisions without getting lost in overthinking. But for now, be kind to yourself. You're doing great, overthinker. Take a breather, practice what you've learned, and we'll be here when you're ready to continue the journey.

Chapter 12: Navigating Major Life Decisions Without Overthinking

I hope you've had a chance to practice some of the techniques we've discussed and are feeling a bit more equipped to handle your overthinking tendencies. Now, let's tackle one of the biggest challenges for any overthinker: making major life decisions.

The Big Decision Spiral

Picture this: You're faced with a life-changing decision. Maybe it's a career change, a cross-country move, or whether to commit to a serious relationship. Suddenly, your brain kicks into overdrive:

"What if I make the wrong choice?"
"What if I regret this decision for the rest of my life?"
"What if there's a better option I haven't considered yet?"

Before you know it, you're caught in a mental whirlpool, analyzing every possible outcome until you're too paralyzed to make any decision at all. Sound familiar?

The Myth of the "Perfect" Decision

Here's the truth bomb: there's no such thing as a perfect decision. Life is too complex, with too many variables, for any decision to be 100% right or wrong. The goal isn't to make a perfect decision, but to make a good enough decision and then make it work.

So, how do we do that? Let's dive into some strategies:

1. The Pro-Con Upgrade

You've probably made pro-con lists before, but let's upgrade this classic tool:

- List your options
- For each option, write out the pros and cons
- Now, rate each pro and con on a scale of 1-10 for importance
- Sum up the scores

This gives you a more nuanced view than a simple list. But remember, this is a tool to inform your decision, not make it for you.

2. The Future Self Consultation

Imagine yourself 5, 10, or 20 years in the future. What would your future self advise you to do? This can help you focus on your long-term values rather than short-term fears.

3. The Worst-Case Scenario Planning

Instead of trying to avoid thinking about the worst-case scenario, lean into it:

- What's the worst that could happen?
- How likely is it to happen?
- If it did happen, how would you cope?

Often, you'll find that even the worst-case scenario is manageable, which can ease your anxiety about deciding.

4. The Values Alignment Check

List your core values (if you're not sure what they are, now's a great time to reflect on this). How does each option align with these values?

Sometimes, the "right" decision becomes clearer when viewed through the lens of your values.

5. The Intuition Tune-In

While data and logic are important, don't discount your gut feeling. After you've done your rational analysis, take a moment to tune into your intuition. Sometimes, your subconscious has processed information your conscious mind hasn't caught up with yet.

6. The Decision Deadline

Overthinkers can get stuck in analysis paralysis. Combat this by setting a decision deadline. Give yourself enough time to thoughtfully consider your options, but not so much time that you spiral into endless research and rumination.

7. The Reversibility Test

Ask yourself: Is this decision reversible? If so, you might feel more comfortable moving forward knowing you can change course if needed. If it's not easily reversible, that's valuable information too.

8. The Trusted Council

Seek advice from people you trust who have your best interests at heart. But be selective—too many opinions can overwhelm an overthinker. Choose 2-3 trusted advisors.

9. The Alternative Universe Exploration

Instead of trying to predict the future, try this: For each option, imagine a scenario where it works out great, and another where it doesn't. This can help you realize that your happiness isn't solely dependent on this one decision.

10. The "Good Enough" Embrace

Remember, you're not looking for the perfect decision, but a good enough decision. Embrace the idea of "satisficing"—finding a satisfactory solution that suffices, rather than an optimal solution that might not exist.

Real-Life Application: My Career Crossroads

Let me share a personal story. In my mid-30s, I was faced with a major career decision: stay in my stable but unfulfilling corporate job, or take a risk and pursue my passion for writing full-time.

My overthinking mind went into overdrive. I made spreadsheets projecting my finances five years into the future. I polled every friend and family member for their opinion. I even started having stress dreams about being a starving artist.

Finally, I used many of the techniques we've discussed. I consulted my future self (who was miserable in the corporate job). I did a values alignment check (creativity and autonomy topped my list). I set a decision deadline.

In the end, I took the leap. Was it scary? Absolutely. Did everything go perfectly? Nope. But it was a "good enough" decision that I could work with, and it led me to where I am today—happier, more fulfilled, and ironically, much less of an overthinker.

Your Decision-Making Mission

The next time you're faced with a big decision, I challenge you to:

1. Use at least three of the strategies we've discussed.

2. Set a decision deadline and stick to it.

3. Once you've made your decision, commit to it fully. Put your energy into making it work rather than second-guessing yourself.

Remember, there's no growth without some discomfort. Making decisions, especially big ones, will always involve some level of uncertainty. But with these tools in your mental toolkit, you're well-equipped to navigate that uncertainty without getting lost in overthinking.

As we wrap up this chapter, take a deep breath. You've got this. You're not just an overthinker—you're a thoughtful, considerate decision-maker. Trust yourself.

In our next chapter, we'll explore how to break the cycle of overthinking in parenting. But for now, celebrate your newfound decision-making skills. You're one step closer to mastering your overthinking mind!

Chapter 13: Parenting and Overthinking: Breaking the Cycle

Hi again, thoughtful parents and parents-to-be! If you've made it this far, you're already well on your way to mastering your overthinking tendencies. Now, let's tackle one of the most anxiety-inducing, second-guess-yourself-at-3am roles out there: parenting.

The Parental Overthinking Trap

Parenting and overthinking go together like peanut butter and jelly - it's a classic combination, but sometimes it's just too sticky. From the moment you become responsible for another human being, your mind can go into hyperdrive:

"Am I doing this right?"

"What if I make a mistake that affects them for life?"

"Should I have chosen a different school/activity/diet/bedtime routine?"

Sound familiar? You're not alone. The good news is, you've already got a solid foundation for managing these thoughts. Let's build on that with a few key strategies tailored for parenting.

Strategy 1: The Parenting Values Compass

Remember our values alignment check from the decision-making chapter? Let's adapt this for parenting. Take some time to identify your core parenting values. Maybe it's kindness, resilience, creativity, or honesty. Whatever they are, write them down.

Now, when you're caught in a parenting dilemma and your mind starts spinning, consult your values compass. Ask yourself: "Which choice aligns best with my parenting values?" This can cut through the noise of overthinking and guide you towards decisions that feel right for your family.

Strategy 2: The "Good Enough" Parenting Embrace

Perfectionism is overthinking's best friend, and it has no place in parenting. Enter the concept of "Good Enough" parenting, coined by pediatrician and psychoanalyst D.W. Winnicott.

The idea is simple: you don't need to be a perfect parent (spoiler alert: there's no such thing). You just need to be good enough. Kids don't need perfection; they need love, attention, and the space to learn and grow.

When you catch yourself spiraling about a parenting decision, ask: "Is what I'm doing good enough?" Chances are, the answer is yes.

Strategy 3: The Parental Self-Compassion Pause

Parenting can be a guilt trip waiting to happen. But remember our self-compassion practice? It's time to put it to work in your parenting life.

When you're beating yourself up over a parenting choice, take a self-compassion pause:

1. Acknowledge the difficulty: "Parenting is hard, and I'm struggling right now."
2. Remember your common humanity: "All parents face challenges and doubts. I'm not alone in this."
3. Offer yourself kindness: "May I be kind to myself in this moment. I'm doing my best."

This simple practice can help break the cycle of parental guilt and overthinking.

Breaking the Overthinking Cycle

Now, here's where things get really interesting. As you work on managing your own overthinking, you're also modeling healthy thought patterns for your kids. You're not just helping yourself; you're potentially breaking an intergenerational cycle of overthinking.

How? Children learn by example. When they see you:

- Pausing before reacting
- Expressing self-compassion
- Making decisions without agonizing
- Admitting mistakes and moving forward

They're learning valuable skills for managing their own thoughts and emotions.

My Parenting Overthinking Journey

When I became a parent, my overthinking went into overdrive. I remember agonizing over every decision, from what brand of diapers to use to which preschool philosophy was best.

One day, as I was spiraling about whether I'd irreparably damaged my child by letting them watch 30 minutes of TV, I caught myself. I took a deep breath and asked, "Is this good enough?"

The answer was yes. My child was happy, healthy, and loved. That was good enough.

From that moment on, I started practicing these strategies. And you know what? Not only did I feel better, but I noticed my child seemed more relaxed too. They were picking up on my calmer energy.

Your Parenting Overthinking Mission

This week, I invite you to:

1. Create your Parenting Values Compass. Refer to it when you're stuck in a parenting dilemma.
2. Practice asking "Is this good enough?" at least once a day.
3. Use the Self-Compassion Pause whenever you notice parental guilt creeping in.

Remember, you're not aiming for perfect parenting (it doesn't exist!). You're aiming for thoughtful, values-aligned, good-enough parenting. And from where I'm sitting, the fact that you're even reading this shows you're already nailing it.

As we wrap up this chapter, take a moment to appreciate yourself. Parenting is tough, and you're doing it while also working on your own personal growth. That's pretty amazing.

In our next chapter, we'll put all the pieces together and create your personal peace plan. But for now, go hug your kids (or yourself). You're doing great, thoughtful parent. Keep going!

Chapter 14: Creating and Maintaining Your Personal Peace Plan

Picture this: You're standing at the helm of a ship called "Your Life." The seas of overthinking have been choppy, but you've navigated through storms of anxiety, whirlpools of indecision, and the occasional kraken of self-doubt. Now, it's time to chart a course for calmer waters. Welcome to your Personal Peace Plan—your map to a life with less overthinking and more tranquility.

By now, you've amassed quite the toolkit for managing your overthinking tendencies. You're no longer a novice sailor; you're the captain of your mental ship. But even the most experienced captains need a reliable map and a solid plan. That's what we're creating today.

The Blueprint for Your Peace Plan

Your Personal Peace Plan isn't a one-size-fits-all solution. It's a customized strategy that takes into account your unique thought patterns, triggers, and goals. Here's how to craft yours:

1. Reflect on Your Journey

Take a moment to look back at how far you've come. What techniques have worked best for you? Which challenges do you still face? This reflection will form the foundation of your plan.

2. Identify Your Overthinking Triggers

We all have specific situations that set our minds racing. Maybe it's work deadlines, social interactions, or making decisions about your kids. List your top three overthinking triggers.

3. Choose Your Go-To Techniques

For each trigger, select one or two techniques from this book that you find most effective. This creates your first line of defense against overthinking spirals.

4. Establish Daily Mindfulness Practices

Consistency is key. Choose one short mindfulness practice you can commit to daily. It might be a 5-minute meditation, a gratitude journal, or a mindful walk. This is your mental maintenance routine.

5. Create an Emergency Toolkit

For those moments when overthinking hits hard, have a list of quick, effective strategies ready. This might include deep breathing exercises, the 5-4-3-2-1 grounding technique, or a favorite affirmation.

6. Set Realistic Goals

What does "less overthinking" look like for you? Set specific, measurable goals. For example, "I want to reduce the time I spend worrying about work in the evenings by 50%."

7. Plan for Setbacks

Setbacks are not failures; they're opportunities for learning. How will you handle days when overthinking gets the better of you? Include self-compassion and resilience strategies in your plan.

8. Schedule Regular Check-Ins

Your needs may change over time. Plan to review and adjust your Peace Plan every month or two.

Putting Your Plan into Action

Now that you have your blueprint, it's time to build. Start small—Rome wasn't built in a day, and neither is a calm mind. Begin by implementing one or two elements of your plan and gradually add more as they become habits.

Remember, this is a living document. As you grow and change, so too will your Peace Plan. Be flexible and kind to yourself as you navigate this new way of thinking.

My Personal Peace Plan Journey

When I first created my Personal Peace Plan, I was skeptical. Could a simple document really help manage years of overthinking habits? But as I consistently applied my plan, I noticed a shift. The change wasn't overnight, but gradually, like a ship changing course, my mind began to steer towards calmer waters.

One key element of my plan was a daily 10-minute meditation. At first, it felt impossible to quiet my racing thoughts. But with practice, those 10 minutes became an anchor in my day, a pause button for my overactive mind.

Your Peace Plan Mission

This week, your mission is to draft your Personal Peace Plan. Don't aim for perfection (remember, we're recovering overthinkers here!). Start with a rough draft and refine it as you go.

Once you've created your plan, commit to following it for the next month. Keep track of your progress, noting what works well and what might need adjusting.

As we near the end of our journey together, take a moment to acknowledge how far you've come. You're not just reading about managing overthinking—you're actively creating a blueprint for a more peaceful mind.

In our final chapter, we'll explore how to maintain your progress and continue growing beyond the pages of this book. But for now, set sail with your new Peace Plan. The shores of a calmer mind are on the horizon, captain. Full steam ahead!

Chapter 15: Embracing a Calmer, More Peaceful Life - Your Ongoing Journey

Congratulations, intrepid thought explorer! You've reached the final chapter of our adventure together. But don't think of this as the end - it's more like graduating from Overthinking University. You're not finished; you're just beginning a new phase of your journey.

The Road So Far

Take a moment to reflect on where you started. Remember that person who picked up this book, desperate for a way to quiet the constant chatter in their mind? That person who felt overwhelmed by decisions, paralyzed by "what-ifs," and exhausted from mental marathons?

Now, look at yourself today. You've gained insights into why your mind works the way it does. You've learned techniques to manage your thoughts, strategies to make decisions, and ways to be kinder to yourself. You're not the same overthinker you were when you started this book.

But here's the thing about personal growth - it's not a destination; it's a journey. So, how do you keep moving forward?

Maintaining Your Progress

1. Consistency is Key

Remember, managing overthinking is like exercising a muscle. The more consistently you practice, the stronger you become. Stick with your Personal Peace Plan, adjusting as needed.

2. Celebrate Small Wins

Did you make a decision without agonizing? Navigate a social situation without overthinking? Celebrate it! Acknowledging your progress reinforces positive change.

3. Practice Self-Compassion

There will be days when overthinking gets the better of you. That's okay. Treat yourself with kindness. You're human, not a robot.

4. Keep Learning

Stay curious about your mind. Continue to read, learn, and explore new strategies. The field of psychology is always evolving, and so can you.

5. Share Your Journey

Consider sharing what you've learned with others. Teaching is one of the best ways to reinforce your own learning.

Continuing to Grow

As you move forward, here are some ways to continue your growth:

1. Join a Support Group

Consider finding a local or online group for recovering overthinkers. Sharing experiences and strategies can be incredibly powerful.

2. Explore Therapy

If you haven't already, consider working with a therapist. They can provide personalized strategies and support.

3. Start a Mindfulness Practice

If you haven't already, consider developing a regular mindfulness or meditation practice. It's one of the most powerful tools for long-term thought management.

4. Keep Journaling

Continue to track your thoughts and progress. It's a great way to spot patterns and celebrate growth. *My High-Level Gratitude Journal* is a great option!

5. Set New Goals

As you master your current goals, set new ones. Maybe you want to apply your new skills to a particular area of your life, like your career or relationships.

My Ongoing Journey

I'll let you in on a secret: I still have days where overthinking creeps in. The difference is, now I have the tools to manage it. I no longer feel at the mercy of my thoughts.

Recently, I faced a major life decision. In the past, this would have sent me into an overthinking spiral. Instead, I used the techniques we've discussed. I consulted my values, used the pro-con upgrade, and set a decision deadline. Was it completely stress-free? No. But it was manageable, and I made a decision I felt good about.

Your Continuing Mission

As we conclude our time together, I have one final mission for you:

Commit to being a lifelong student of your mind. Set an intention to check in with yourself regularly, to continue using the tools you've learned, and to be open to new strategies as you discover them.

Remember, the goal isn't to never overthink again. The goal is to have a healthier relationship with your thoughts, to use your analytical skills as a superpower rather than a limitation.

Final Thoughts

You've come so far, and I'm incredibly proud of you. Remember, every time you catch yourself overthinking and choose a different path, you're rewiring your brain. You're creating new neural pathways that lead to a calmer, more peaceful way of being.

As you close this book, know that you have everything you need within you to continue this journey. You're equipped with tools, strategies, and most importantly, a new understanding of your incredible mind.

So go forth, thoughtful one. Embrace your analytical nature while enjoying the peace that comes with managing it effectively. You've got this. And on the days when you don't feel like you've got it, remember - that's just a thought, and you now know exactly what to do with those.

Here's to your calmer, more peaceful life. It's been an honor to be part of your journey.

Bonus Chapter: Words of Wisdom - A Motivational Pick-Me-Up

Welcome to your personal reservoir of inspiration and wisdom. In the journey of overcoming overthinking and cultivating a positive mindset, sometimes we all need a little boost. This chapter is designed to be your go-to source for motivation, a place to turn when you need to realign your thoughts or find that extra push to keep going.

Here, you'll find a collection of original quotes alongside wisdom from some of the world's greatest thinkers. Whether you're facing a moment of doubt, need a reminder of your strength, or simply want to reinforce your positive mindset, these words are here to guide and inspire you.

Feel free to bookmark this chapter, highlight your favorites, or even write them down to keep with you. Remember, every great journey begins with a single step, and sometimes, that step is simply shifting your perspective. Let these words be the wind beneath your wings as you soar towards a calmer, more peaceful mind.

On Overthinking:

"Overthinking is like rocking in a rocking chair. It gives you something to do, but it doesn't get you anywhere."

"Your mind is a powerful thing. When you fill it with positive thoughts, your life will start to change."

"Overthinking: the art of creating problems that weren't even there."

"Don't believe everything you think. Thoughts are just that - thoughts."

"Overthinking is the habit of trying to control things you can't."

"Overthinking is like a hamster wheel—lots of energy expended, but no forward movement."

"The mind is a wonderful servant, but a terrible master."

"Overthinking is the evil twin of planning."

"Not everything that pops into your mind deserves a five-star accommodation."

"Overthinking is like quicksand - the more you struggle, the deeper you sink."

"The primary cause of unhappiness is never the situation but your thoughts about it." - Eckhart Tolle

"Worry is like a rocking chair: it gives you something to do but never gets you anywhere." - Erma Bombeck

On Mindset:

"Your mindset is your personal weather forecast. Choose sunshine."

"A positive mindset isn't about expecting the best to happen every time, but accepting that whatever happens is the best for this moment."

"Your mind is like a garden. You can grow flowers or you can grow weeds. The choice is yours."

"Mindset reset: breathe in courage, exhale doubt."

"A calm mind is the ultimate weapon against your challenges."

"Your mindset is the lens through which you view the world. Keep it clean and clear."

"A positive mindset is not about being happy all the time. It's about knowing you can handle whatever comes your way."

"Your mindset is like a muscle - the more you train it, the stronger it becomes."

"Change your mindset, change your life. It's that simple, and that difficult."

"A growth mindset is the fertilizer for success."

"Whether you think you can, or you think you can't—you're right." - Henry Ford

"The mind is everything. What you think you become." - Buddha

On Self-Compassion:

"Be as kind to yourself as you are to your best friend."

"Self-compassion is not self-indulgence. It's self-preservation."

"You're allowed to be both a masterpiece and a work in progress simultaneously."

"Loving yourself isn't vanity. It's sanity."

"Treat yourself like someone you're responsible for helping."

"Self-compassion is the foundation upon which all personal growth is built."

"You can't pour from an empty cup. Take care of yourself first."

"Self-compassion is giving yourself the same kindness and care you'd give to a good friend."

"The most powerful relationship you will ever have is the relationship with yourself."

"Self-compassion turns self-criticism from a weapon into a tool."

"You yourself, as much as anybody in the entire universe, deserve your love and affection." - Buddha

"Be gentle with yourself, learn to love yourself, to forgive yourself, for only as we have the right attitude toward ourselves can we have the right attitude toward others." - Wilferd Peterson

On Resilience:

"You've survived 100% of your worst days. You're doing great."

"Resilience isn't about never falling down. It's about getting up one more time than you fall."

"The oak fought the wind and was broken, the willow bent when it must and survived." - Robert Jordan

"Rock bottom can be a great foundation on which to build a better life."

"You are stronger than you think. You are more capable than you know."

"Resilience is knowing that you are the ocean, not the wave."

"The human spirit is like a rubber band: the further you stretch it, the greater it snaps back."

"Resilience is the art of bouncing forward, not just bouncing back."

"Life doesn't get easier or more forgiving; we get stronger and more resilient."

"Resilience is the secret ingredient in the recipe of success."

"I can be changed by what happens to me. But I refuse to be reduced by it." - Maya Angelou

"The human capacity for burden is like bamboo - far more flexible than you'd ever believe at first glance." - Jodi Picoult

On Growth:

"Growth is painful. Change is painful. But nothing is as painful as staying stuck somewhere you don't belong."

"The only way to make sense out of change is to plunge into it, move with it, and join the dance." - Alan Watts

"Every next level of your life will demand a different you."

"Comfort is the enemy of progress."

"The greatest discovery of all time is that a person can change their future by merely changing their attitude." - Oprah Winfrey

"Growth is the only evidence of life."

"The seed of greatness is planted in discomfort."

"Personal growth is not a matter of learning new information but unlearning old limits."

"The biggest room in the world is the room for improvement."

"Growth and comfort do not coexist. Choose wisely."

"There is no growth without change, no change without fear or loss, and no loss without pain." - Rick Warren

"The only way that we can live, is if we grow. The only way that we can grow is if we change. The only way that we can change is if we learn. The only way we can learn is if we are exposed. And the only way that we can become exposed is if we throw ourselves out into the open. Do it. Throw yourself." - C. JoyBell C.

Remember, these words are here for you whenever you need them. Let them be a lighthouse guiding you through the stormy seas of overthinking to the calm waters of a peaceful mind. Your journey to a calmer, more focused you is ongoing, and every step forward is a victory. Keep growing, keep learning, and most importantly, keep believing in yourself.

Take your gratitude to the next level...

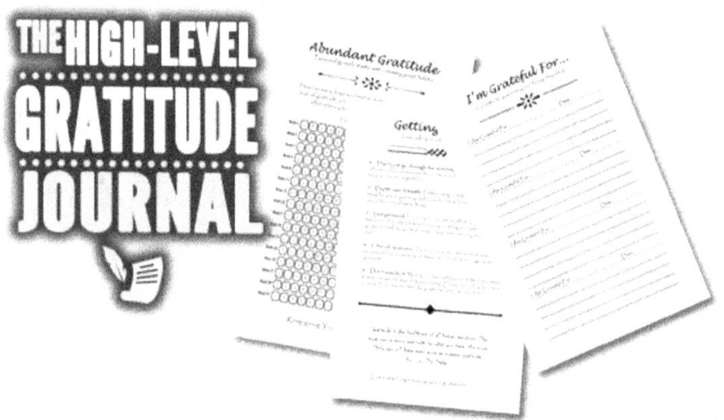

High-Level Gratitude Journal

The Super Silly Gratitude Journal For Kids

Thank you for reading *Clam Your Chaos*. I truly appreciate you giving my book a chance. If you have any questions, connect with me at my website, www.tormentpublishing.com.

Acknowledgements:
Special thanks to Torment Publishing! Without you
this book would not have happened. I love you guys.
Thanks to all my family for the support!

122

Credits:
David R. Bernstein – Publishing & Marketing Support